Piano Technique

Book 4

T0028157

Authors
Barbara Kreader, Fred Kern, Phillip Keveren, Mona Rejino

Director, Educational Keyboard Publications
Margaret Otwell

Editor	*Illustrator*
Carol Klose	Fred Bell

Book: ISBN 978-0-634-01356-0
Book/CD: ISBN 978-0-634-08977-0

HAL•LEONARD®
CORPORATION
7777 W. BLUEMOUND RD. P.O. BOX 13819 MILWAUKEE, WI 53213

Visit Hal Leonard Online at
www.halleonard.com

Dear Teacher,

Piano Technique Book 4 presents a *Warm-Up* and an *Etude* for each new technical skill students will encounter in **Piano Lessons Book 4**.

We suggest that you demonstrate each *Warm-Up*. Teaching by demonstration allows students to focus on the purely physical aspects of learning a new skill, such as hand and body position, or arm and finger movement. This helps them understand the connection between the movement they make and the sound they create.

Once students have learned the physical skill presented in each *Warm-Up*, they can use it to play the corresponding *Etude* with expression.

The *Musical Fitness Plan* on each warm-up page teaches new technical concepts and provides a checklist for technical readiness:

- **Changing Positions**
- **Playing Black-key/ White-key Combinations**
- **Crossing 2 over 1**
- **Playing One Hand *Legato* and the Other *Staccato***
- **Syncopation between the Hands**
- **Syncopated Pedaling**
- **Tucking 1 under 3 and Crossing 3 over 1**
- **Crossing One Hand over Another**
- **Playing Blocked and Broken Chords in Close Position**
- **Crossing 2 over 1 to a Black Key**
- **Combining Musical Skills**
- **Playing Left-hand Melody and Right-hand Accompaniment**
- **Sustaining One Note while Playing Another Note in the Same Hand**
- **Substituting One Finger for Another**
- **Extending to an Octave**

By the end of **Piano Technique Book 4**, students will be able to play the C and G Major and A and E Minor scales, and the I, IV, V7, I chord progression in root and close positions, both blocked and broken. Having learned all these skills, students will have the confidence to move on to the technical challenges presented in **Piano Lessons Book 5**.

Best wishes,

Barbara Kreader   *Fred Kern*

Phillip Keveren   *Mona Rejino*

Dear Students,

You need an exercise plan to stay physically fit.

Like participating in sports, playing the piano is a physical activity that uses your whole body. **Piano Technique Book 4** will outline the *Musical Fitness Plan* you need to develop new musical skills.

Your *Musical Fitness Plan* includes:

- **Warm-Ups** – drills to develop new musical skills
- **Etudes** – music to practice using the new skills you learned in the *Warm-Ups*

It feels good to play the piano! Your teacher will show you how to play each *Warm-Up*. Follow the *Musical Fitness Plan*, paying careful attention to the way you use your body, arms, and fingers to create music. When you play, notice how the movement you make affects the sound you create. Once you have learned each *Warm-Up*, read and practice the matching *Etude*.

You are now ready to begin.

Have fun!

Barbara Kreader   *Fred Kern*

Phillip Keveren   *Mona Rejino*

Piano Technique Book 4

CONTENTS

* Students can check activities as they complete them.

Musical Fitness Review

Use the following checklist to demonstrate the skills you learned in **Book 3**.

☐ **Playing in Extended Position**
Sometimes it is necessary to extend outside a five-finger position to play a note above or below that position. Let your hand expand slightly as you shift outward with either your thumb or your fifth finger.

☐ **Playing Chords**
Listen for each chord tone to sound at exactly the same moment. Drop into each chord with the full weight of your arm, balancing it equally over each finger.

☐ **Using the Damper Pedal**
Press the damper pedal down with your right foot, keeping your heel on the floor.

☐ **Changing Positions**
When moving from one position to another, use your thumb or fifth finger as a guide. Look ahead. Plan your move to a new position.

☐ **Playing Black-key/White-key Combinations**
When playing either melodic or harmonic intervals using a black-key/white-key combination, move your hand slightly forward for comfort.

Major Minor
Review Etude

Using all the confidence you gained in **Piano Technique Book 3**, celebrate your new musical skills!
Play each five-finger pattern with a downward motion of the arm, ending with an upward motion of the wrist.

Use with Lesson Book 4, pg. 4

Musical Fitness Plan

Use this checklist to review fitness skills and to focus on learning new ones.

☐ **Playing in Extended Position**

☐ **Changing Positions**

☐ **Playing Black-key/White-key Combinations**

NEW!

Crossing 2 over 1
As you cross finger 2 over 1, gently rotate your wrist toward your thumb, keeping your thumb in place.

NEW!

Playing One Hand *Legato* and the Other *Staccato*
In one hand, pass the sound from finger to finger. At the same time in the other hand, release the key as soon as you play it.

To the Teacher: Demonstrate these warm-ups first. This will allow students to focus on the purely physical aspects of learning a new skill. Encourage students to play each warm-up in different octaves.

Warm-Ups

Red Rover *pg. 8*

*"Red Rover,
Red Rover,
May finger two
cross over?"*

*Have you ever
played "Red Rover?"
Players stand in two lines of equal number and hold hands.*

One line chants the words above, calling out the name of a member of the opposing line. That player comes running at full speed and tries to "cross over" and break through the line of chanters.

Extend one note beyond the range of a five-finger pattern by crossing your second finger over your first.

As you cross finger 2 over 1, gently rotate your wrist toward your thumb, keeping your thumb in place. As soon as you play finger 2, return it to its original position.

Get It Together *pg. 9*

Do you remember the first time you tried to walk and dribble a basketball at the same time? Walk across the room bouncing an imaginary ball. Notice how the downward motion of your hand and foot happen at the same time.

Imitate this coordination as you play **Get It Together**. The left hand begins the walking movement and the right hand enters its bouncing notes at the same time the left hand finishes.

Tap and count:

R.H.

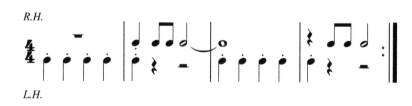

L.H.

Red Rover

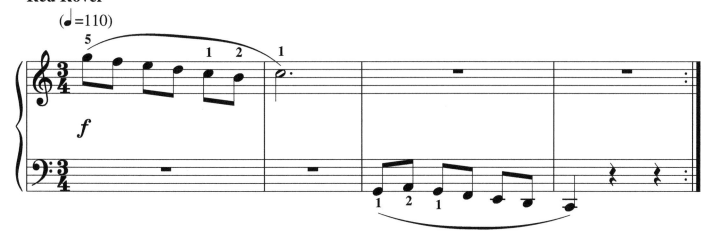

Get It Together

Red Rover

Get It Together

Moderato (♩=120)

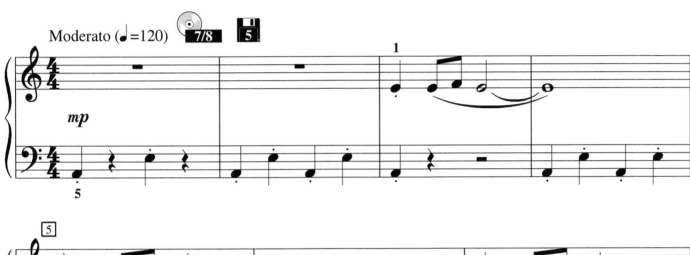

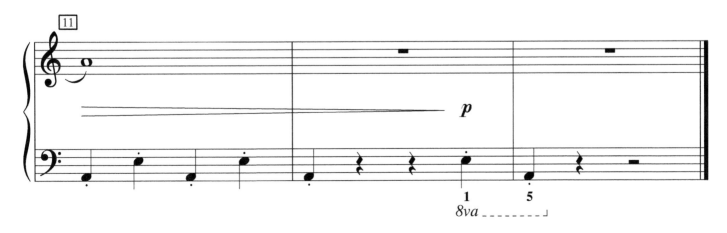

9

Use with Lesson Book 4, pg. 6

Musical Fitness Plan

Use this checklist to review fitness skills and to focus on learning new ones.

☐ **Playing in Extended Position**

☐ **Playing Chords**

☐ **Changing Positions**

Syncopation Between Hands
Tap syncopated rhythms away from the keyboard, saying the hand combinations out loud, either "right," "left," or "together."

NEW!

Syncopated Pedaling
Place the ball of your right foot on the damper pedal, keeping your heel on the floor. Lower and raise the pedal with the ball of your foot according to the pedal markings.

Pedal at exactly the right moment, neither too late nor too soon. Listen carefully. There should be no blur or break in the sound.

To the Teacher: Continue to demonstrate these warm-ups first. Encourage students to create variations by moving the warm-ups to different octaves or transposing them to different keys.

Warm-Ups

Take It Away *pg. 12*

9 **6**

Today we use calculators to solve math problems. In ancient China, people used an abacus, a frame with sliding beads. If they wanted to subtract two from four, for example, they started with a full count of four beads, slid two beads away, and then counted the remaining beads.

It is possible to solve the technical difficulties of playing syncopated rhythms in a similar way. **Take It Away** begins with both hands playing on all of the strong beats, then takes away beats by tying them over to create the syncopation.

Tap and count:

Bell Choir *pg. 13*

10 **7**

Have you ever heard or played handbells? Sometimes two or more bells ring together, blending their sounds. Most of the time, though, each player keeps the sound of his or her bell from overlapping with the next by stopping the sound. Timing is important.

When playing **Bell Choir**, clear the sound between chords by pedaling at exactly the right moment, neither too soon nor too late. Listen carefully so you make no blur or break in the sound.

Take It Away

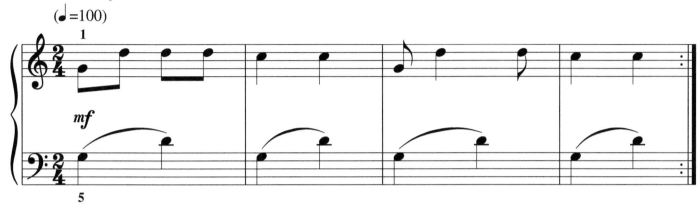

Bell Choir

1. First practice pedaling without playing. Place your right foot on the damper pedal and keep your heel on the floor. Lower and raise the pedal as you count "1 & 2 & 3 & ." Use the pedal markings and arrows as a guide.

2. Now play the warm-up below, lowering and raising the pedal as you continue to count the eighth-note pulse. Notice how you lower the pedal on "&" and raise it on "1," creating the effect of syncopation. Using the pedal in this way is called **syncopated pedaling**.

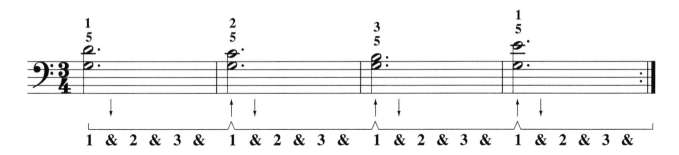

Take It Away

Spirited ($\quarternote$=120)

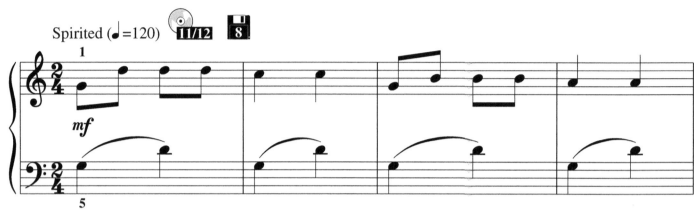

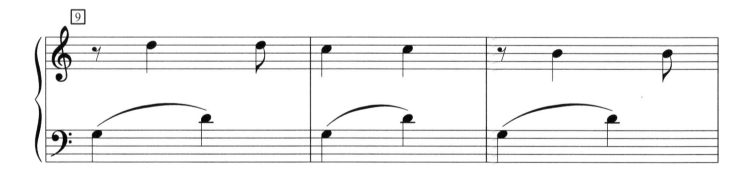

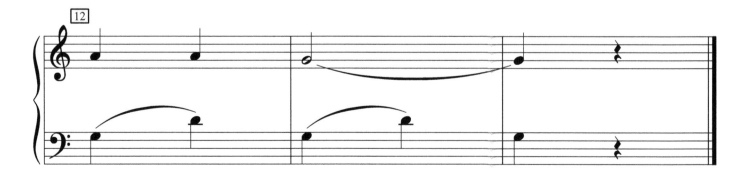

Bell Choir

With energy (♩=120)

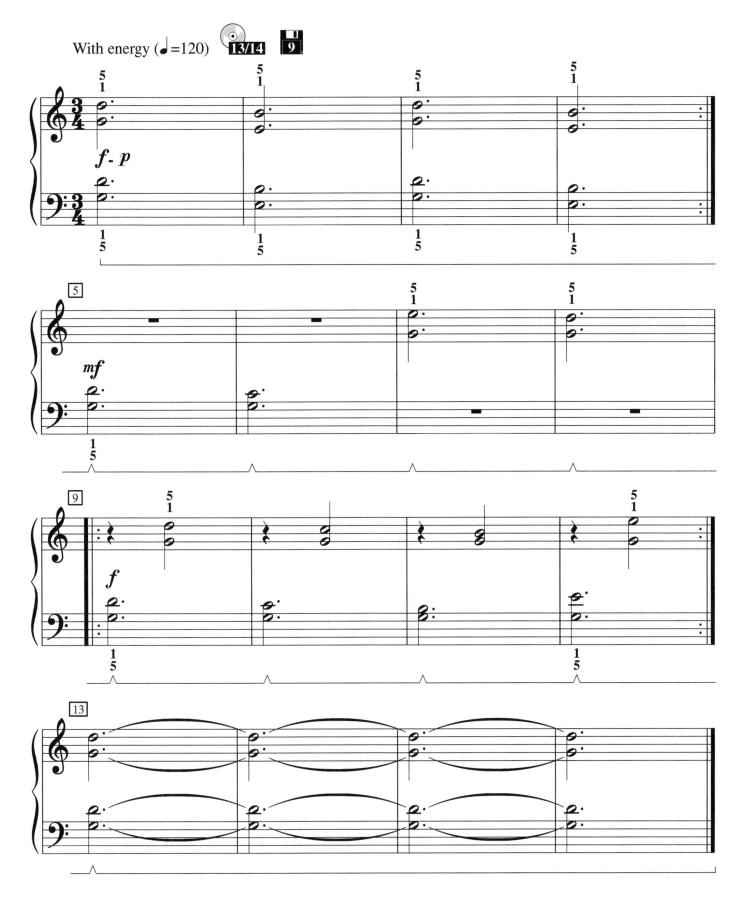

Use with Lesson Book 4, pg. 9

Musical Fitness Plan

Use this checklist to review fitness skills and to focus on learning new ones.

- ☐ **Playing in Extended Position**

- ☐ **Changing Positions**

- ☐ **Playing Black-key/White-key Combinations**

Tucking 1 under 3
When playing scales (R.H. ascending/L.H. descending), tuck your thumb under your third finger. As soon as you play your thumb, move fingers 2-3-4-5 to their new positions. Let your arm guide your fingers smoothly up and down the keyboard, keeping your wrist level as you play each scale.

Crossing 3 over 1
When playing scales (R.H. descending/L.H. ascending), let your wrist and forearm follow through as you cross your third finger over your thumb. As soon as you play finger 3, move fingers 2-1 to their new positions. Let your arm guide your fingers smoothly up and down the keyboard, keeping your wrist level as you play each scale.

To the Teacher: Continue to demonstrate these warm-ups first. Encourage students to create variations by moving the warm-ups to different octaves.

Warm-Ups

Silk And Satin *pg. 16*

15 🖫10

Fill a bag with various pieces of fabric – silk, burlap, lace, tapestry. Close your eyes and reach into the bag. Try to identify the type of cloth you choose.

When you make the transition from one hand to another, imagine you are running your fingers along a fine silk scarf. Listen for a smooth sound. Measure the distance of each left-hand interval carefully. During the half rests, move each hand to its next position.

Zip It *pg. 17*

16 🖫11

When you zip your coat, you pull the zipper in one continuous motion up or down, letting your arm guide your fingers.

Let your arm guide your fingers smoothly up and down the keyboard as you play each scale. Prepare to play each one by first practicing the thumb movements alone. When you have mastered those, play the entire scale.

For right-hand ascending or left-hand descending scales, tuck your thumb under your third finger. Move your arm, hand, and fingers to their new position as soon as you play the thumb.

When playing a left-hand ascending or right-hand descending scale, let your wrist and forearm follow through as you cross your third finger over your thumb. Release your thumb the moment you play it, moving your hand, arm, and fingers into position for fingers 3, 2, 1 to play the remaining notes of the scale.

Silk And Satin

($\quad$= 80)

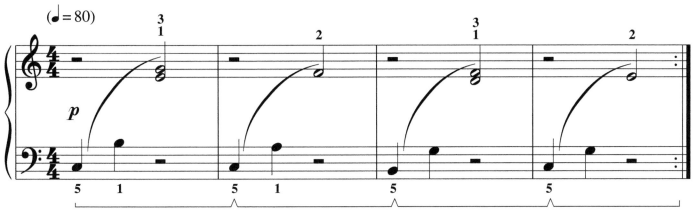

Zip It!

($\quad$=100)

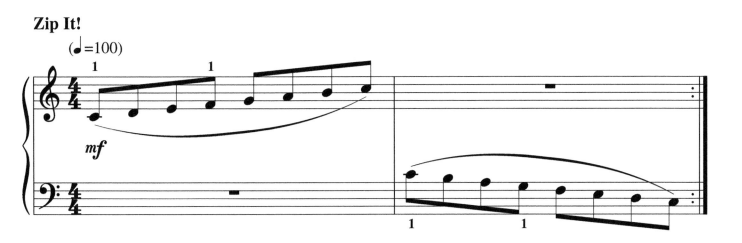

Silk And Satin

Smoothly ($\quad$ = 90)

Play both hands one octave higher throughout.

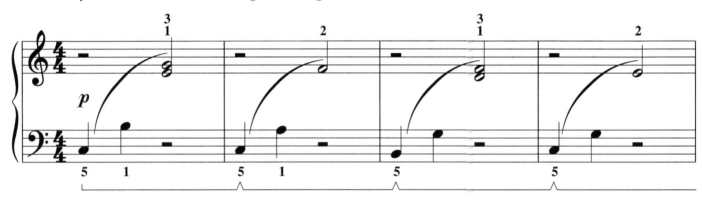

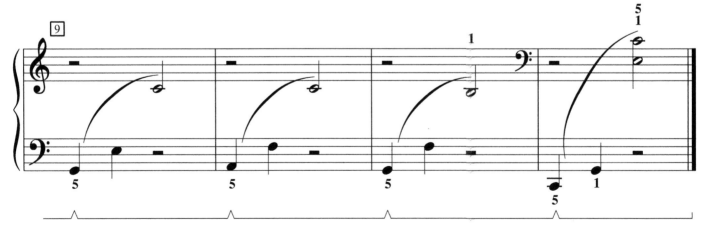

Zip It!

Happily (♩=110)

Use with Lesson Book 4, pg. 13

Musical Fitness Plan

Use this checklist to review fitness skills and to focus on learning new ones.

Crossing One Hand over Another
When crossing one hand over the other, use one continuous, arching motion. To move from hand to hand without creating a break in the sound, begin moving one hand to its new position while the other is playing.

☐ **Combining Musical Fitness Skills**
 • Playing in Extended Position
 • Changing Positions
 • Playing Chords
 • Playing Black-key/White-key Combinations

To the Teacher: *Continue to demonstrate these warm-ups first. Encourage students to create variations of the warm-ups by moving them to different octaves.*

Warm-Ups

Bungee Cord *pg. 20*

(21) [14]

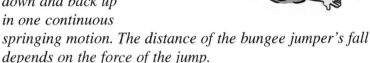

Bungee cords move down and back up in one continuous springing motion. The distance of the bungee jumper's fall depends on the force of the jump.

Place your *left hand* in the C Major five-finger pattern. Practice moving your *right hand* in a smooth arc back and forth from middle C (thumb) to bass G (third finger). Play with one continuous motion, moving from hand to hand without a break in sound.

Beethoven's Fifth – Not! *pg. 21*

(22) [15]

When you are getting ready for school, you have to do many things quickly – pack your lunch, find your homework, brush your teeth, fill your backpack, find your bus money, remember your music. You have to do each task on time so you won't be late.

Beethoven's Fifth – Not! asks you to make split-second position changes in each hand. Keep alert at all times, using the rests to make your moves. Think: *move-prepare-play.*

Bungee Cord

($\quad . = 64$)

Place both hands in the C position before you begin.

Keep your left hand in position as you play the right hand notes in measures 1, 3, 5, and 7.

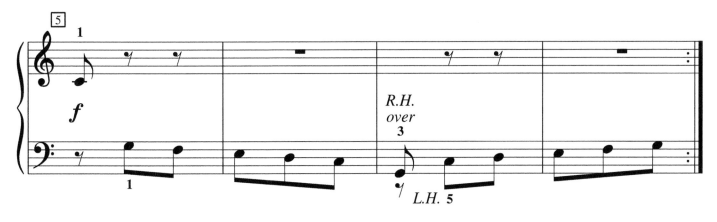

Beethoven's Fifth – Not!

($\quad = 115$)

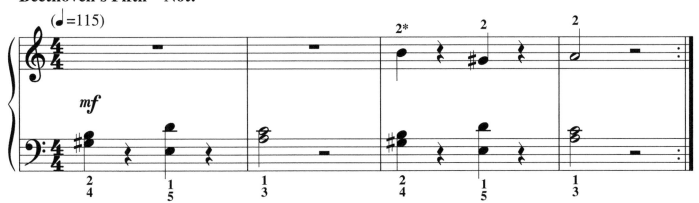

This fingering outlines the position changes in Gurlitt's Allegro.

19

Bungee Cord

Beethoven's Fifth – Not!

*This fingering outlines the position changes in Gurlitt's Allegro.

21

Musical Fitness Plan

Use this checklist to review fitness skills and to focus on learning new ones.

- ☐ **Playing in Extended Position**

- ☐ **Changing Positions**

- ☐ **Tucking 1 under 3**

- ☐ **Crossing 3 over 1**

NEW!

Playing Blocked Chords in Close Position
When moving from one chord to another, gently reach with the thumb or fifth finger to the outside chord tones. Pay close attention to the fingering for the middle chord tone so you will maintain a comfortable hand position.

NEW!

Playing Broken Chords in Close Position
Use the same fingering to play blocked or broken chords in close position. Flex your wrist gently from side to side. Play each broken chord with one down/up motion of your wrist and arm.

Warm-Ups

Reaching *pg. 24*

27 **18**

When you reach for some-thing on the top shelf of your closet, you keep your toes on the floor as you extend your upper body and arms.

When moving from chord to chord, prepare ahead for the next position. Keep the common tone (bottom note) in place. To play the top note, gently reach with either your left-hand thumb or your right-hand fifth finger. Pay close attention to the fingering you use for the middle note. This will help you keep a comfortable hand position.

Smooth Hand-Off *pg. 25*

28 **19**

Members of a relay team learn to hand the baton from one runner to the next without losing any momentum. The next runner stands ready to run with his or her hand in position to receive the baton.

Prepare each hand to play its scale while the other is completing its "run." Pass the sound smoothly from hand to hand with one continuous motion.

Reaching

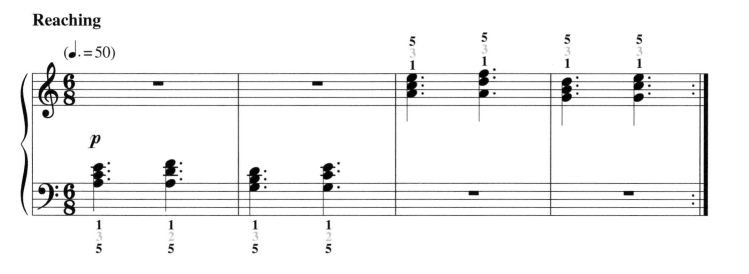

Smooth Hand-Off

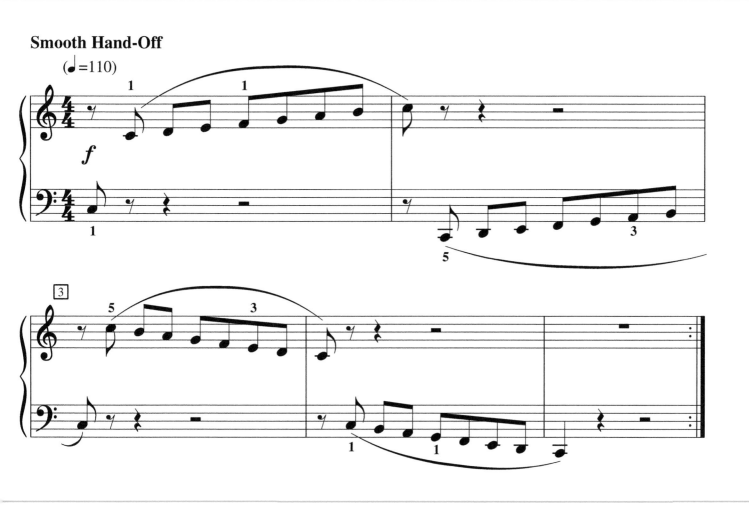

Reaching

Smoothly (♩. = 60)

Smooth Hand-Off

Musical Fitness Plan

Use this checklist to review fitness skills and to focus on learning new ones.

☐ **Playing in Extended Position**

☐ **Changing Positions**

☐ **Playing Chords**

NEW!

Crossing 2 over 1 to a Black Key
When crossing 2 over 1 to a black key, move your hand slightly forward for comfort. Play your thumb on its outside tip.

To the Teacher: Continue to demonstrate these warm-ups first. Encourage students to create variations of them by transposing them to different keys.

Warm-Ups

Hurry Up And Wait *pg. 28*

Think about those days when you are so hungry that you hurry to the lunch room. Much to your frustration, you arrive to find a long line. You can either spend the time feeling upset by the delay or relaxing as you talk to a friend.

Music imitates these hurry-up-and-wait moments when it includes lots of rests. Relax your arm weight during each one, counting the resting pulses carefully.

Keep in mind that the right notes at the wrong time are still wrong! During a rest, carefully prepare your move from one interval or chord to another.

Tidal Lullaby *pg. 29*

When you first arrive at the beach, the sound of the tide captures your attention. After you swim and sun for awhile, the ebb and flow of the waves becomes a reassuring background pulse. Your attention turns to the individual sounds of children laughing, dogs barking, and people talking.

Play the left-hand patterns with a flexible wrist, passing the sound from finger to finger. Use your second finger as the pivot point. When you can play the left-hand patterns smoothly, concentrate on bringing out the sound of the right-hand melody. Lean into each melody note, keeping your arm weight behind each finger. Create a rise and fall of the dynamics within each phrase.

Hurry Up And Wait

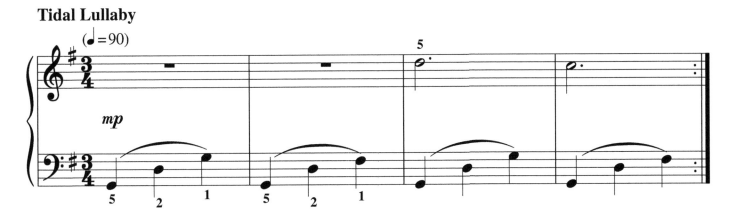

Tidal Lullaby

27

Hurry Up And Wait

Moderato (♩=130)

1st time both hands one octave higher.

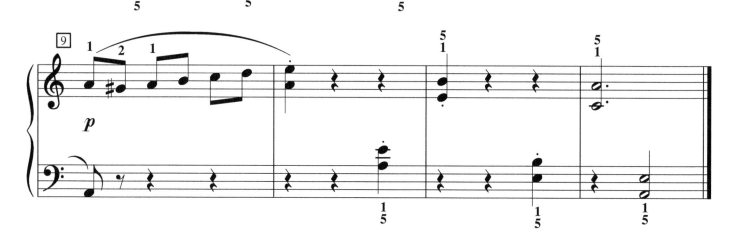

Tidal Lullaby

Rocking (♩=100)

Use with Lesson Book 4, pg. 31

Musical Fitness Plan

Use this checklist to review fitness skills and to focus on learning new ones.

☐ **Combining Musical Skills**
- Playing in Extended Position
- Playing Chords
- Changing Positions
- Playing Black-key/White-key Combinations

To the Teacher: Continue to demonstrate these warm-ups first. Encourage students to create variations of the warm-ups by moving them to different octaves.

Warm-Ups

Talkin' To My Left Hand *pg. 32*

39 **26**

Sometimes the best way to learn a subject, such as multiplication facts or spelling words, is to recite them aloud. In this way, you give directions to yourself.

One important technical skill involves keeping your thinking ahead of your playing. By saying the words in **Talkin' To My Left Hand**, you tell your left hand what to do *before* you play the notes. The words help you focus on the finger numbers you will be using for each interval.

When playing an interval that uses a black-key/white-key combination, move your hand slightly forward for comfort.

Heading For Home *pg. 33*

40 **27**

When you are on third base, you keep your eyes on home plate and run for it. You don't pay much attention to the ground in between, and you stop only when you arrive at the plate.

The triplets in **Heading For Home** lead to the main beats. Say the words of the title as you play each triplet group. Don't let the notes trip over each other! Play each triplet with a clean, even sound, giving the quarter notes more emphasis.

Talkin' To My Left Hand

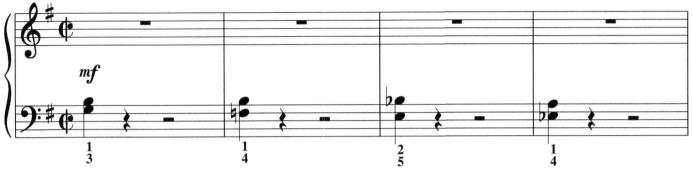

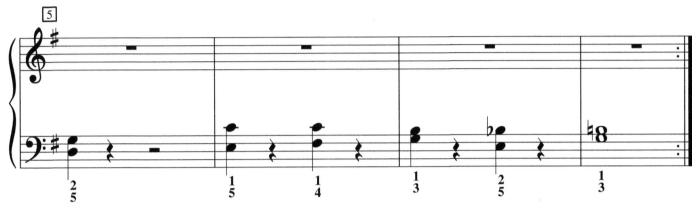

Heading For Home

Talkin' To My Left Hand

Slowly (♩=50)

Words spoken in rhythm.

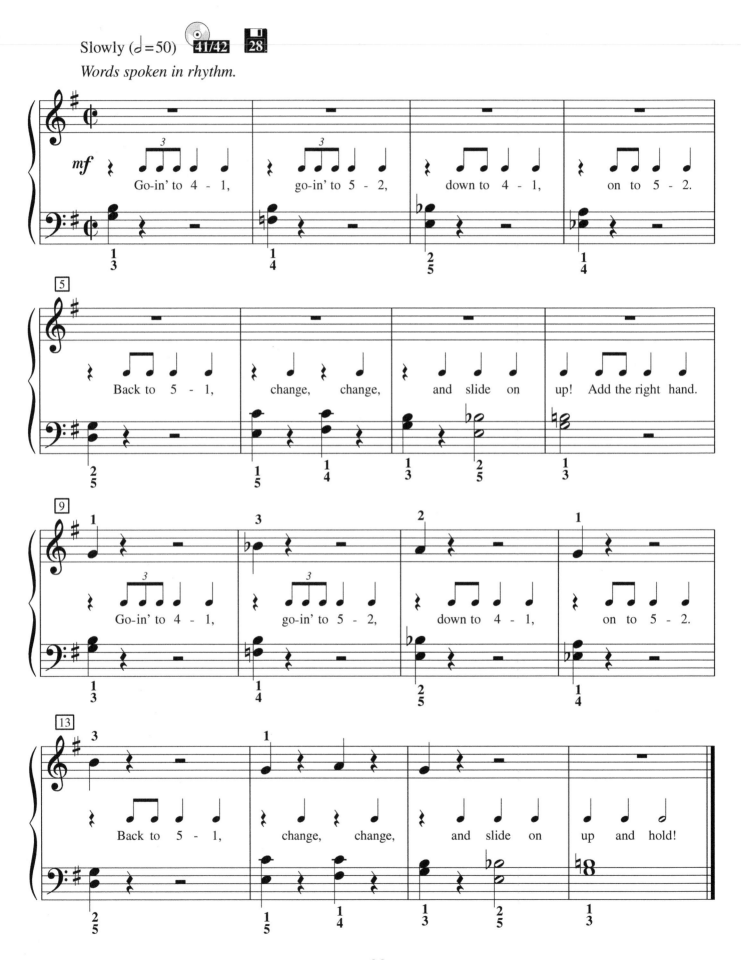

Heading For Home

Use with Lesson Book 4, pgs. 34-35

Musical Fitness Plan

Use this checklist to review fitness skills and to focus on learning new ones.

☐ **Playing in Extended Position**

☐ **Changing Positions**

☐ **Playing Chords in Close Position**

☐ **Crossing 2 over 1**

☐ **Playing One Hand** *Legato* **and the Other** *Staccato*

NEW!

Playing a Left-hand Melody and Right-hand Accompaniment
Give a left-hand melody emphasis by leaning into each key with more arm weight than you use for the right-hand accompaniment.

Warm-Ups

Fitting In *pg. 36*

Think about a family car trip. Sometimes two children ride in the back seat, but occasionally three must fit into the same space! You might complain, "He's not fitting in!" Your mother might reply, "Well, try harder!"

Tap a quarter-note pulse as you chant the words:

"Fit-ting in.   Fit-ting in.   Try to fit in.   Try to fit in!"

As you play the etude **Fitting In**, pass the sound smoothly from finger to finger during each phrase. Gently move your right-hand thumb outside the five-finger pattern to reach the notes in measures 10-11 and 14-15.

Low-Down *pg. 37*

When someone gives you the "low-down," they tell you the basic facts about a situation. They focus only on what you need to know and spare you any extra details.

The left hand has the "low-down" in this etude. Give the left-hand notes emphasis by playing them with more arm weight than you use for the right-hand notes. Release the eighth-note chords with a gently bouncing wrist.

Fitting In

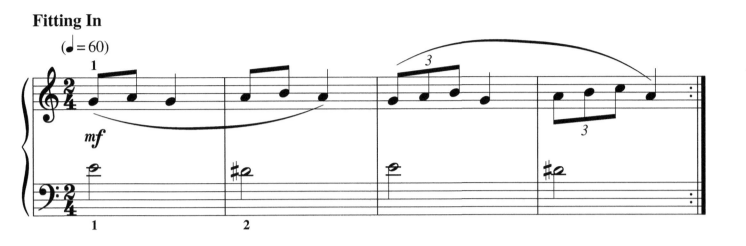

Low-Down

Fitting In

Adagio (♩ = 66) **47/48** **32**

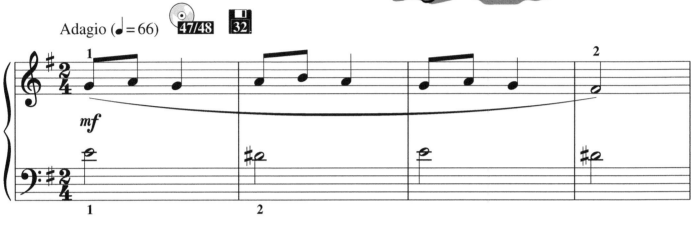

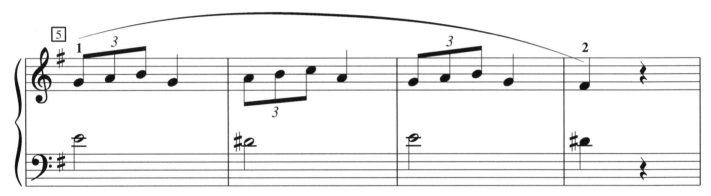

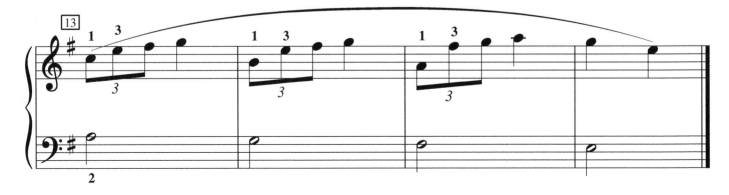

Use with Lesson Book 4, pg. 37

36

Low-Down

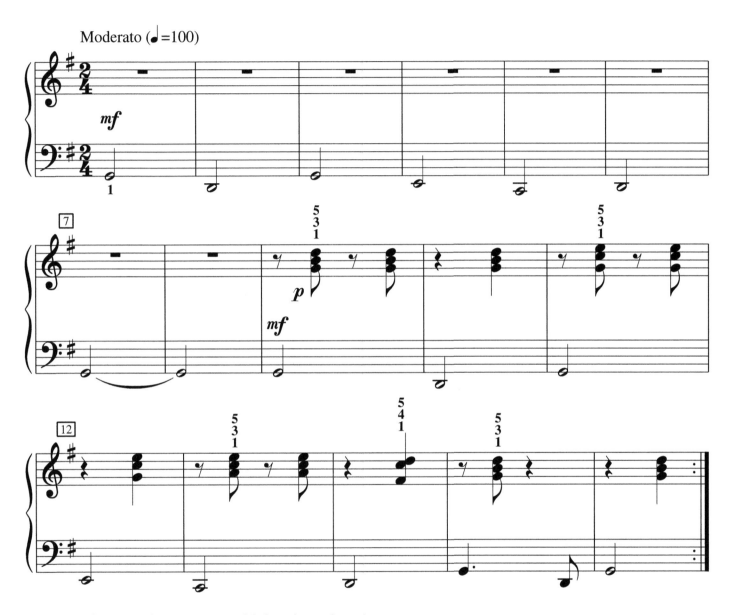

Accompaniment (Play one octave higher throughout.)

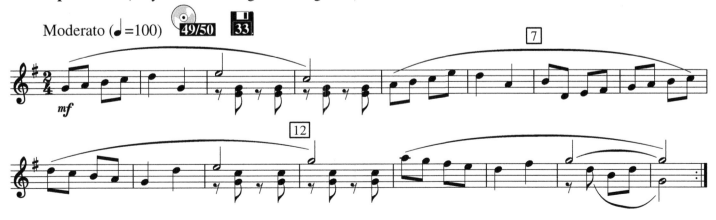

Use with Lesson Book 4, pg. 39

Musical Fitness Plan

Use this checklist to review fitness skills and to focus on learning new ones.

☐ **Playing in Extended Position**

☐ **Changing Positions**

☐ **Playing Black-key/White-key Combinations**

☐ **Syncopated Pedaling**

Sustaining One Note while Playing Another Note in the Same Hand
Sustain the lower note by pressing the key to the bottom of the keybed. Play the other note using a light, floating touch.

Substituting One Finger for Another
To reposition your hand on a repeated note, substitute one finger for another. Keep your fingers close to the keys so you can make a quick change.

Warm-Ups

In A Swing *pg. 40*

When you give yourself a push on a swing, you send yourself floating effortlessly into the air. You feel the strongest pull at the lowest point of the swing. Then you soar higher and let your legs sail out in front of you.

When you play the two-note pattern in the left-hand part, play the second note lightly with the thumb. Be sure to hold the first note of each measure for three beats.

Beach Ball *pg. 41*

When you toss a beach ball from hand to hand, you gently move it from one side of your body to the other.

When you "toss" a four-note phrase from hand to hand, play each group of notes with one drop/lift motion of your arm and wrist. Make the notes in one hand sound exactly like those in the other.

If you give the ball a slight shove and your friend catches it, you feel a toss-and-hold rhythm.

When you play a four-note broken chord followed by a harmonic interval, follow through smoothly from one hand to the other.

In A Swing

Beach Ball

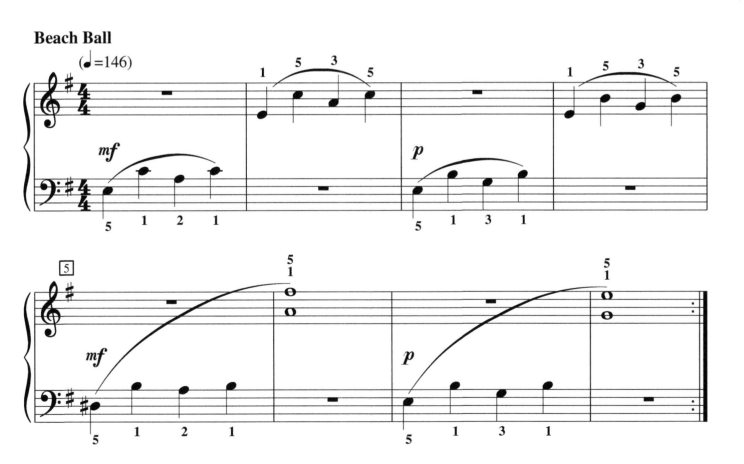

In A Swing

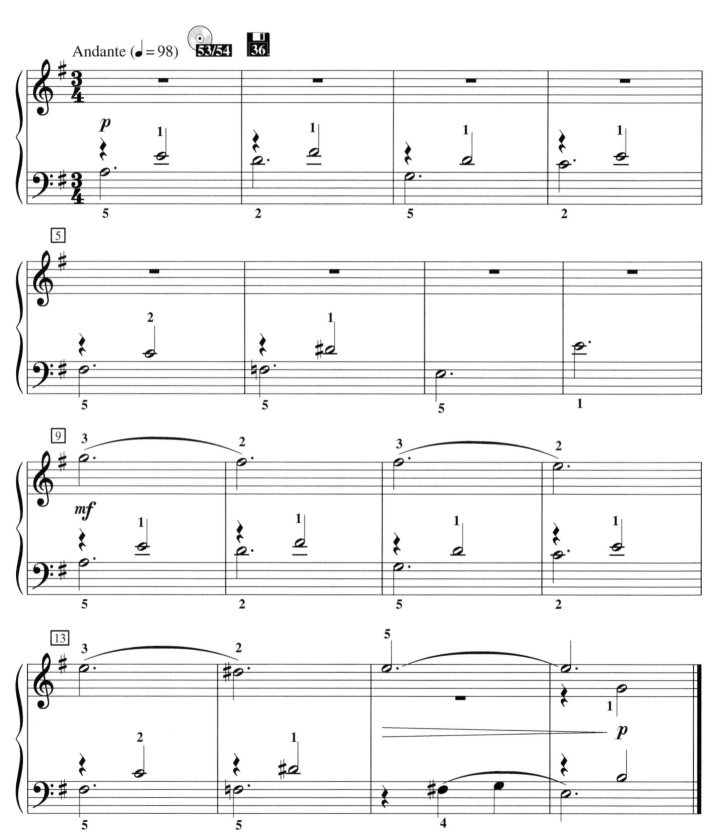

Beach Ball

Allegro (♩=166)

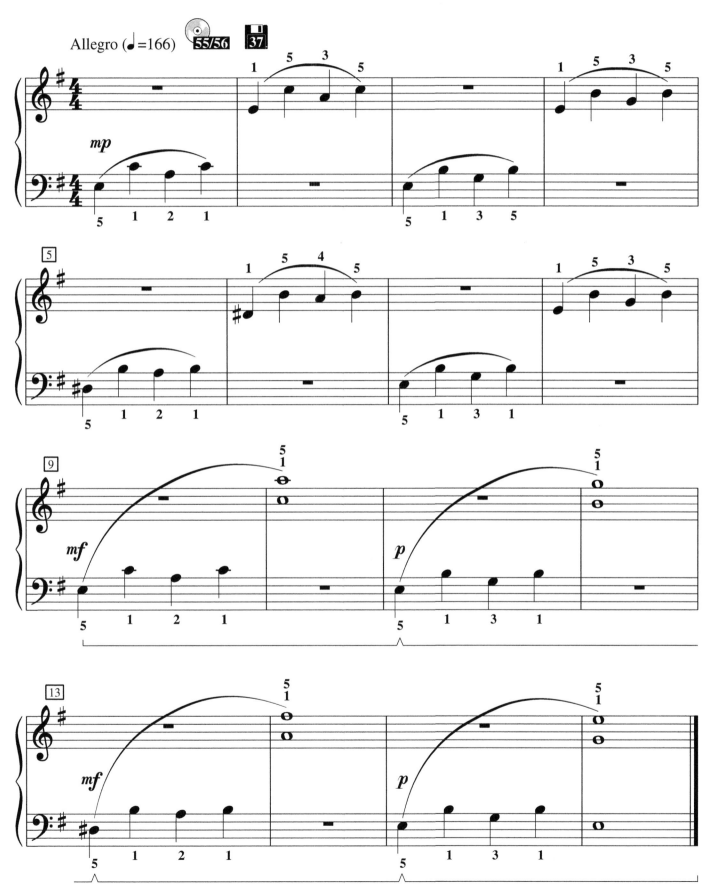

Use with Lesson Book 4, pgs. 42-43

Musical Fitness Plan

Use this checklist to review fitness skills and to focus on learning new ones.

☐ **Playing in Extended Position**

☐ **Playing Chords**

☐ **Changing Positions**

☐ **Playing Black-key/White-key Combinations**

☐ **Crossing 2 over 1**

☐ **Syncopated Pedaling**

☐ **Sustaining One Note while Playing Another Note in the Same Hand**

☐ **Substituting One Finger for Another**

To the Teacher: Continue to demonstrate these warm-ups first. Encourage students to create variations of the warm-ups by moving them to different octaves.

Warm-Ups

Kaleidoscope *pg. 44*

57 💾 **38**

When you turn the end of a kaleidoscope, you treat yourself to a display of continually changing geometric patterns in a full spectrum of colors.

The etude **Kaleidoscope** presents continually changing intervals and sequences in a full spectrum of dynamic shadings. Pay attention to the common tones from one interval to the next, moving only those fingers that change. Use the same fingering for every left-hand sequence, playing each one with a drop/lift motion of the arm and wrist.

Rolling Down The Hill *pg. 45*

58 💾 **39**

Can you remember what it feels like to roll down a hill? You give yourself a big push and watch the world turn upside down as you turn over and over in one continuous motion.

Play all five notes in one drop/lift motion of your arm and wrist without blurring or breaking the sound. Pass the notes from finger to finger. Use a slight rotation of your wrist to give the notes momentum.

Kaleidoscope

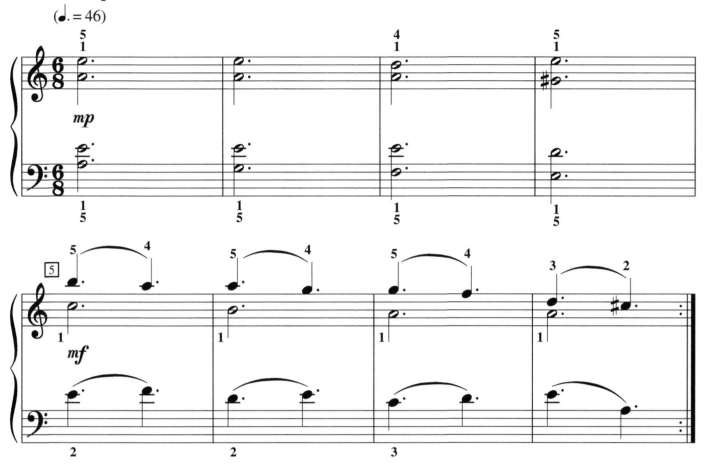

Rolling Down the Hill

Kaleidoscope

Andante (♩. = 46) **59/60** **40**

Rolling Down The Hill

Rolling along (♩=140)

Use with Lesson Book 4, pg. 45

Musical Fitness Plan

NEW!

Extending to an Octave
When a pattern covers the range of an octave, keep your hands relaxed, flexing your wrist gently from side to side as you play and release the lowest and highest notes.

☐ **Changing Positions**

☐ **Combining Musical Fitness Skills**

Warm-Up

Horn Call *pg. 47* 🔢63 💾42

When the brass section of an orchestra sounds a dramatic fanfare, they play chord tones with majesty. Trumpet and trombone players can play notes that cover a large intervallic range with fingering that is easier than the one pianists have to use when playing the same music.

Each two-measure pattern covers the range of a seventh or an octave. Keep your hands relaxed, with your second and third or fourth fingers resting on the keys they will play in each pattern. Flex your wrist gently from side to side as you play and release the lowest and highest notes in each pattern, balancing your hand over the second and third or fourth fingers.

Horn Call
($\mathbf{\frac{1}{2}}$ = 60)

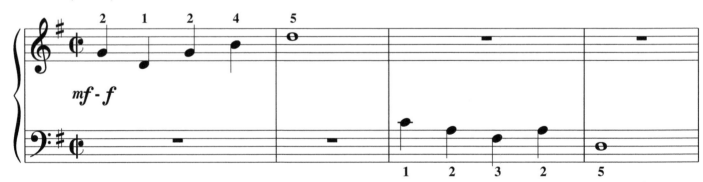

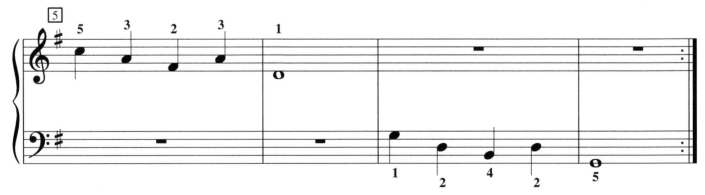

Horn Call

Use with Lesson Book 4, pg. 46

Scales

Play these exercises, first hands separately and then hands together, in the following keys:

C Major   G Major   A Minor   E Minor

Practice each $\frac{4}{4}$ exercise in the following tempi: ♩ = 72; ♩ = 80; ♩ = 88; ♩ = 100; ♩ = 120.

Practice the $\frac{6}{8}$ exercise in the following tempi: ♩. = 88; ♩. = 100; ♩. = 120.

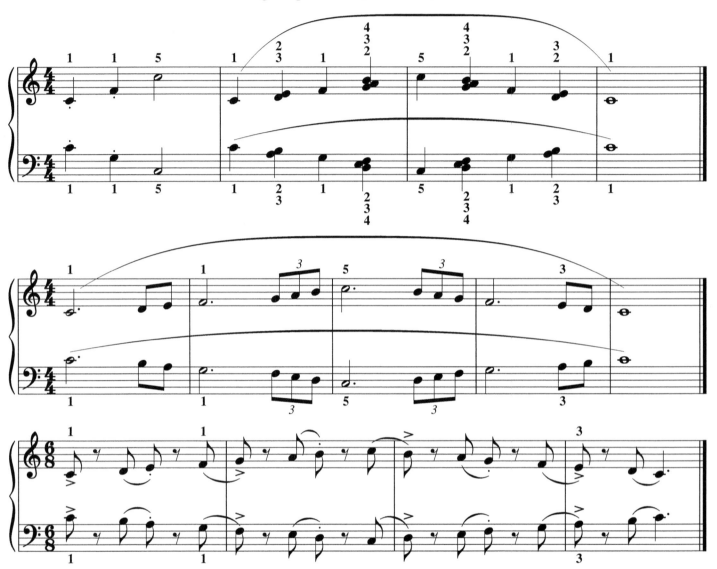

Play the unstemmed notes in one quick impulse *before* each beat, using a drop/lift motion of the wrist.

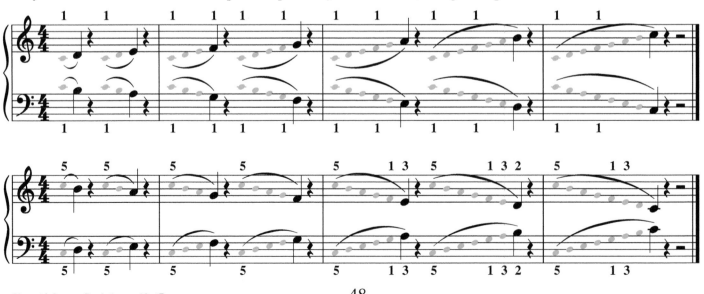